A YEAR OF POSITIVITY JOURNAL

A YEAR OF
POSITIVITY
JOURNAL

52 Weeks of Prompts and Practices to Cultivate a Positive Mindset

EVELYN BETANCES

ROCKRIDGE
PRESS

First Rockridge Press trade paperback edition 2022

Rockridge Press and the Rockridge Press logo are trademarks or registered trademarks of Callisto Media Inc. and/or its affiliates in the United States and other countries and may not be used without written permission.

For general information on our other products and services, please contact our Customer Care Department within the United States at (866) 744-2665, or outside the United States at (510) 253-0500.

Paperback ISBN: 979-8-88608-014-8

Manufactured in the United States of America

Interior and Cover Designer: Sean Doyle
Art Producer: Megan Baggott
Editor: Marjorie DeWitt
Production Editor: Jax Berman
Production Manager: Martin Worthington

Illustration © iStock, cover; Author photo courtesy of Emily Kim

10 9 8 7 6 5 4 3 2 1 0

This Journal Belongs to:

_____

CONTENTS

INTRODUCTION

Hi there! I'm Evelyn Betances, and I'm so glad you decided to join me on this journey. I'm a life coach specializing in mindset transformation. My whole life, I've been drawn to helping people work through difficult situations and emotions. Individuals would come to me with their problems—I think it was because I listened calmly, never passed judgment, and was always warm and friendly.

As a speaker, strategist, and mindset transformation coach, I want to encourage individuals to stand in their power. I am the founder and CEO of the Fab Chieftess brand; our purpose is to inform and inspire others to reclaim their authority, boost confidence, address impostor syndrome, and overcome fear so that they can bring their aspirations to life.

Prior to launching my company, I served as a program manager for high-profile clients. As an ambitious go-getter, I had a plan for my life and often pushed myself to achieve my career and financial goals. In my work, I was surprised to see intelligent, capable, and highly successful people not reaching their potential because of issues with perfectionism and impostor syndrome. They let the "you can't have it all" motto impede their progress on many fronts.

I pursued coaching as a way to make things better for people. I created a company, developed a brand, and launched the She Minds app. My goal was to educate, empower, build community, and positively impact the world around me. By merging my corporate skills, life experiences, and passion, I have created a space to serve clients who lack vision and are often overwhelmed.

Today, I work with individuals from all walks of life to help them create positive shifts. I hope you've found your way to these pages because you're looking for guidance and support on your journey to becoming a happier and grounded person. Alternatively, maybe this was a gift from someone who cares about you and wants to help. Either way, I hope you'll stick with me as I encourage you on your journey toward positivity. Now, I know what you're thinking: "There's no way this book is going to change my life." And that may be true. You're right that a book can't change your life all on its own. But it can give you the tools to change your own life; you just have to put in a little legwork.

Over the years, I have developed a number of tools that help my clients deal with one of their biggest obstacles, their own minds. This journal is designed to help you develop greater positivity in your life. Positivity isn't just what makes us feel good; it's what boosts our resilience and allows us to face whatever challenges come our way, small or large. So, let's get started.

Note: This journal is not a replacement for medication or medical treatment, but it can be a great supplement. If you're struggling with complicated and debilitating feelings like depression or anxiety, know that there's no shame in seeking treatment from a licensed therapist or medical professional.

Onward to a more positive state.

HOW TO USE THIS BOOK

So, you've decided to start a journaling practice, but how do you plan to start and continue the practice? I'm here to help!

A Year of Positivity Journal is divided into fifty-two weeks, with each week including an affirmation, three prompts, and a practice. The affirmation will set the tone and shift your mindset. The three prompts will allow you to dive deeper into thought and inspire your journaling practice. The last activity, the practice, allows you to take action and build the habit.

One of the best things is that this is a living document: every week, you'll be developing and evolving positive habits. It is completely up to you when you want to work on your journaling practice. Some people like to write during their morning walk, others will record their thoughts during downtime at work, and others will write at the end of the day.

I know that it can feel like an uphill climb at first, but I promise that if you follow my advice and complete one section per week (a month or more of positivity), you'll be well on your way to a more positive future.

52 WEEKS OF POSITIVITY JOURNALING

RELATIONSHIP TO THE SELF

My relationship with myself is becoming stronger, deeper, and more loving so I can evolve and develop my higher self.

It all starts with you and the relationship you have with yourself. What does your self-relationship look and feel like? What would you like that relationship to evolve into?

_____

_____

_____

_____

_____

_____

_____

It is important to build on and care for the relationship you have with yourself. Can you think of areas where you can improve the care in your self-relationship? What can you do on a daily, weekly, and monthly basis?

_____

_____

_____

_____

_____

_____

_____

How people care for others can influence how they care for themselves. Are there any glaring differences between how you care for others and the care you give yourself?

_____

_____

_____

_____

_____

_____

_____

Think of something you have really wanted to do that will spark great joy while allowing you to develop a closer and more loving relationship with yourself. It can be a small or big action. For example, maybe you've always wanted to take a solo road trip or sign up for mind/body classes.

WEEK 2

MY ENERGY

I cherish and am in alignment with my feminine energy. There is strength and wisdom in embracing this energy and in holding space for its evolution.

Every person has both masculine and feminine energy forming two parts of the whole. Feminine energy is nurturing, soft, grounded with boundaries, and trusting of intuition. It is the opposite of masculine energy, which is logical and focused. Individuals can express both no matter their gender. It's common that people neglect their feminine energy because of societal influence. What is your relationship with your feminine energy?

_____

_____

_____

_____

_____

_____

Envision an aura (the visual representation of energy around a person or thing) that would represent your feminine form. What colors and feelings come to mind?

_____

_____

_____

_____

_____

_____

Feminine and masculine energy can cross over and share similarities just as much as they can be different. How do these energies differ or relate for you? How do they complement each other?

_____

_____

_____

_____

_____

_____

_____

Create a vision board; either digital or print will work. Use this board to bring the inspiration for your ideal feminine form to life. The world is your oyster. Use pictures, words, audio, and video: anything that evokes the sense of feminine self and energy you envision. Most importantly, make sure this vision board is easily accessible and visible.

YOUR INSPIRATION

I inspire and am inspired. I am an inspiration to those around me. I matter, and what I have to offer also matters.

You are an inspired individual. Let's focus on the areas where you are most inspired. In what areas do you commonly feel the most inspired (i.e., career, relationships, health)?

_____

_____

_____

_____

_____

_____

_____

Dive a little deeper now. What specifically inspires you in those areas? Maybe this is an individual or group of individuals. Maybe it is the environment. Maybe it is how it makes you feel.

_____

_____

_____

_____

_____

_____

_____

Challenges and discomfort cause us to grow. Is there an area that inspires you but that you nonetheless find challenging or uncomfortable? Brainstorm how you will change that.

_____

_____

_____

_____

_____

_____

_____

I want you to create a connection. Take what inspires you and share it with another person (family, friend, colleague, or partner). You can do this in person, via phone/video, or even through social media. You might also connect with someone who shares your inspiration and nurture that relationship.

THE INNER DIALOGUE

I am worthy of self-love, I am worthy of empathy, and I am worthy of kindness. The care I provide for myself is equal to or more than that which I provide to others.

People are often not conscious of the inner dialogue in their minds, which can be judgmental or negative. What does your negative inner dialogue sound like? Pay attention to the nuances. Are the messages similar, and do they follow a pattern?

_____

_____

_____

_____

_____

_____

The habit of negative self-talk is hard to break. What triggers your positive and negative inner monologue? What can you do to ensure more positive self-talk?

_____

_____

_____

_____

_____

_____

Most often, the inner dialogue is influenced or triggered by fear. However, fear is not always negative, because it can keep you safe, heighten your awareness, or motivate you to overcome an obstacle. What are you afraid of and how is that influencing your inner dialogue?

_____

_____

_____

_____

_____

_____

_____

People are often not kind or compassionate to themselves. Today, I want you to take control of that inner dialogue that is not always kind. Create a list of the negative thoughts that come to mind and for each, write two positive thoughts that counter the negativity.

MORNING JOY

I am the sole architect of my life. I choose and design all it encompasses as well as its structure.

The sun is shining and you have opened your eyes from a restful slumber. What are the things that excite you and bring joy to your day?

_____

_____

_____

_____

_____

_____

If you could change something in your morning routine that would allow you to start your day off on a positive note, what would that look like? How do you think that would impact your day?

_____

_____

_____

_____

_____

_____

Pause and give some thought to your morning routine. Is your routine full of activities focused on you or others? Who or what dictates your morning routine? Sometimes external influences can derail plans. Are you encountering this issue?

_____

_____

_____

_____

_____

_____

_____

Create a list of your morning routine activities. Review your final list and perform a thorough and honest assessment about the things that bring positivity to your morning. Remove anything from the list that does not bring positivity to your morning. Then change your routine to match your list. Be sure to think through how you can tailor your routine to increase your motivation and feelings of joy. Remember, you are the architect.

EVOLUTION

*I believe in my ability to overcome all setbacks,
and I practice my skills each day to build
for my successes.*

You are continuously evolving and you aren't the same person that you were yesterday. What are some of the positive changes you have experienced in your life?

_____

_____

_____

_____

_____

_____

_____

Now look at the changes you thought were negative but have turned out to have a positive impact on your life. What key lessons can you take away from these experiences?

_____

_____

_____

_____

_____

_____

Aspire to continue evolving and changing in big ways. What changes do you want to see for yourself, your life, career, and relationships? Some of these changes may be prompted by this journal.

_____

_____

_____

_____

_____

_____

_____

Spend some time thinking about your growth and what that means to you. Is there a course you have your eye on that will develop a skill set? Is there a new hobby you want to try? Do you have something that you are good at and want to take to the next level? Take the first step today.

FIND YOUR STRENGTH

I draw from my inner strength and light, and I focus on my breathing to ground myself and connect to my present state and environment.

When are you most at peace? When do you feel grounded? Hold on to that feeling and think about how you can create more of these moments.

_____

_____

_____

_____

_____

_____

_____

What are the things that you are doing today that help you in the practice of feeling grounded? Are there any triggers that impede your grounding practice? Tap into the feelings you experienced moments ago.

_____

_____

_____

_____

_____

_____

_____

Imagine your future. Future you is happy, at peace, and fully grounded. What do you need to do now to create this future? Do you need to make changes in your life or surroundings?

_____

_____

_____

_____

_____

_____

_____

Meditation has many benefits. It can improve your self-awareness and ability to be present and supports positive emotions. Start with guided meditation focused on your breath. This form of meditation focuses on the rhythm of your breath to help you enter a deeply relaxed state as well as providing a feeling of being grounded and aware of your surroundings and the present moment.

GRATITUDE FOR YOUR BODY

I am grateful for the body I am blessed with. It allows me to live life to the fullest and vibrates with health and energy.

Our bodies are wondrous marvels, and they work hard in helping us achieve. In what ways are you most grateful for your body?

_____

_____

_____

_____

_____

_____

People often focus on the negative aspects or traits of their bodies. Our purpose on this day is to celebrate the positive. What are the best things about your body?

_____

_____

_____

_____

_____

_____

It is important to be mindful of your body and to care for it. On a scale of 1 to 10, with 10 being the most positive response, how would you rate your current body care? Describe your rating.

_____

_____

_____

_____

_____

_____

_____

Reward or challenge: The choice is yours. If you choose "reward," do something as thanks to your body, maybe a massage or a spa day. If you choose "challenge," do something to push your physical boundaries, maybe a flexibility class, dance class, or any form of exercise in which you don't usually participate.

WEEK 9

ENLIGHTENMENT OF THE BODY

My body is a source of strength, inspiration, and love. I am grateful and thankful for how it has allowed me to live life and arrive where I am today.

Our bodies are a true source of wonder. Think of it as an advanced piece of machinery working harmoniously to allow you to live life. How does your body allow you to live your life?

_____

_____

_____

_____

_____

_____

Think about the moments in life when you were unkind to your body or less than grateful for it. In thinking about this, what type of feelings or emotions come up for you?

_____

_____

_____

_____

_____

_____

Now take those feelings and emotions and reframe them for the positive. What do you wish you had done differently in those moments when you were unkind or less than grateful?

_____

_____

_____

_____

_____

_____

Create a more loving relationship with your body. Stand in front of a mirror. Be as exposed as you wish to be (nude or wearing anything that makes you comfortable). Address each of your parts one by one out loud and declare your thanks for the blessings each part has afforded you.

WEEK 10

FORGIVENESS

I am forgiving. I forgive myself and I forgive others for the actions of the past and actions in the future.

Forgiveness is often a difficult concept for many people. What are your thoughts on forgiveness? Are you more apt to forgive? Or do you withhold your forgiveness?

_____

_____

_____

_____

_____

_____

_____

People tend to carry around baggage for longer than needed, essentially sweeping the associated feelings under the proverbial rug. Dig deep. What are some negative emotions or grudges you are still holding?

_____

_____

_____

_____

_____

_____

_____

In what ways do you think you could help yourself with forgiveness? I find that talking things through with someone else helps. Is there someone you feel you could talk to about forgiveness? How would you start that conversation, and what outcome are you looking for?

_____

_____

_____

_____

_____

_____

_____

To grow in your state of forgiveness, it is always good to start small. Recognize the value of forgiveness and how it can improve your life. Identify what needs healing and who needs to be forgiven and for what. Consider joining a support group or seeking a counselor. Acknowledge your emotions about the harm done to you and how it affects your behavior, and work to release them.

MANAGING ANGER

I replace my anger with understanding and compassion. I fully accept responsibility for the consequences of my emotions and actions I may have taken.

Anger is a natural and normal emotion for everyone. The important part is how you act in moments of anger. Who are you when you are angry and how does it manifest into action?

_____

_____

_____

_____

_____

_____

_____

Anger can be a quick emotion to appear for some more than others. In your case, how prone are you to anger? Is it frequent or infrequent? Why do you think you lean toward one or the other?

_____

_____

_____

_____

_____

_____

_____

You are in control of your anger, and your anger does not define or impact who you are as a person. What are the actions you can take to manage the form your anger takes?

_____

_____

_____

_____

_____

_____

Create a plan of action to positively address your anger when it arises. Having a plan will lower the chance of having a negative or impulsive reaction and will prepare you for angry moments. If you're in the moment and talking to someone, maybe you can excuse yourself and say you'll talk about this matter later. When you step away, what actions can you take to calm yourself? Maybe it's a bath, hike, or a few minutes with your favorite music playlist.

EXPERIENCES

*All that I need comes to me and I am
a better person because of my hardships
and achievements.*

People are a culmination of experiences, positive and negative. Take a moment to remind yourself of all the positive experiences that have inspired growth and made you feel amazing. What is a major experience you've had and how did it affect you?

_____

_____

_____

_____

_____

_____

_____

Building on the previous prompt, what are two or three highly impactful experiences you have had that you want to re-create for yourself? Why?

_____

_____

_____

_____

_____

_____

_____

While life experiences have shaped you into the person you are today, they should not define or limit you. Is there a past negative experience holding you back? If so, how can you move beyond it?

_____

_____

_____

_____

_____

_____

_____

Make a plan. The plan can be loose for now, but commit to fleshing it out further as you continue your journal practice. Look at the experiences you wrote about in the second prompt. Make a plan for how you intend to bring these experiences to life and what a potential time line to make that experience tangible looks like. Build in accountability to yourself or to someone else who will help you stay on track.

PRAISE NEEDS NO APPROVAL

I am much more than adequate. I am phenomenal, and I give myself permission to develop the mindset to praise myself.

You'd be surprised how many people neglect tooting their own horn. If you don't, who will? Like Rihanna says, "Shine bright like a diamond." What makes you shine like a diamond?

_____

_____

_____

_____

_____

_____

_____

I bet you are amazing at so many things. Maybe you're great at karaoke, an amazing cook, a great artist, an awesome dancer, etc. Whatever it may be, have you truly given yourself the credit for these gifts? What are you great at doing?

_____

_____

_____

_____

_____

_____

_____

Are you now finding it easier to praise yourself? What are positive praises you have received from others (family, friends, colleagues, partner)?

_____

_____

_____

_____

_____

_____

_____

I believe in the healing power and impact of music. Do you have a motivational playlist? Whether you do or don't, today is the day to create or update your music playlist. Add to this playlist all the songs that make you feel empowered, strong, and praiseworthy. Then jam out.

PERSONA

I am adaptable, self-reliant, persistent, conscious, and creative with everything that I touch, say, or do.

Everyone has strengths and weaknesses whether acknowledged or not. However, it is important to recognize them and develop an adaptable and resilient persona. How do you use your resilience and adaptability to enhance your strengths and diminish weaknesses?

_____

_____

_____

_____

_____

_____

Think about your background and experiences. Do you feel that your background (culture, environment, education) has influenced your life, work, and relationships? How so?

_____

_____

_____

_____

_____

_____

As people evolve, grow, and experience change, the things that they value and find important also change. What are your top three personal values? What is most important to you today?

_____

_____

_____

_____

_____

_____

_____

Personality quizzes and similar self-assessment tools can provide insight and serve as a basis for considering what your special adaptive abilities might be. Please note that such quizzes and self-assessments—which are abundant online and are sometimes administered in the workplace— are of variable validity, but they can be a useful starting point for self-exploration.

CHARACTER TRAITS

I have the type of personality that exudes charisma, confidence, energy, enthusiasm, and excitement because I am true to my identity.

What are the top three things you like most about yourself? Why these three things?

_____

_____

_____

_____

_____

_____

Personality traits are characteristic of enduring behavioral and emotional patterns, rather than isolated occurrences. What are some of the characteristics that comprise your wonderful personality (courageous, loyal, honest, etc.)?

_____

_____

_____

_____

_____

_____

You are the author and hero of your story. What is the plot and name of the superhero movie you are starring in? Get creative and give your story the flair it deserves.

_____

_____

_____

_____

_____

_____

_____

Treat yourself! You are awesome on the inside, so let's match that to the outside. Think about your personality and the persona who embodies the leading role in the movie of your life. Now create an outfit and image that corresponds. Use your existing clothes, hair, makeup, and whatever makes you feel amazing to create your image.

RESOLUTION

*I am a problem solver who
easily manages and finds a solution
to any given problem.*

You are stronger and more adaptable than you think. Think about at least one example of a problem you found challenging and the steps you took to solve it. How did it feel?

_____

_____

_____

_____

_____

_____

In the previous prompt situation, were there things you did that improved your perception of yourself? Did anyone else witness your resolution and provide positive feedback?

_____

_____

_____

_____

_____

_____

Values play a big part in engagement and interaction with our environment and others. What were your top three life values when you were younger? Have they changed over time?

_____

_____

_____

_____

_____

_____

_____

Take a moment to celebrate. Just like it is important to self-praise, it is also important to celebrate all victories, big or small. Celebration can look and feel different for every person so pick something that speaks to you. Enjoy a fancy cup of coffee, spend a day reading a book, or go out for a fancy dinner.

WEEK 17

INNER AND OUTER CONFIDENCE

The presence of my outer self matches my inner self. I am well groomed, healthy, and full of confidence.

On a scale of 1 to 10, with 10 being the most positive response, how would you rate your confidence level? What impacts this value?

_____

_____

_____

_____

_____

_____

_____

With this in mind, how do you feel about the current value you have assigned? There is always room for growth. What can you do to increase your confidence rating?

_____

_____

_____

_____

_____

_____

What are the top three things you find most valuable about your grooming ritual, your health, and your confidence? Make sure to think of three things for each.

_____

_____

_____

_____

_____

_____

Expand on your health and presence rituals as a way to further build your confidence. Build a vision board of inspiration on Pinterest. To start, go to Pinterest.com and create an account, if you don't have one already. Create a board that will inspire and motivate you to build on your routine. Fill it with self-care ideas, confidence quotes, new activities, and new ways to bring self-care into your routine.

TRIGGERS

I focus only on the good in others. I attract positive and confident people because I am one of those people.

People attract other people who have the qualities that they wish to see in themselves. What types of people have you been attracting lately? What kind of qualities do they possess?

_____

_____

_____

_____

_____

_____

_____

Sometimes people attract things, situations, or other people that can trigger uncomfortable feelings or create a negative visceral reaction. When is one time that you attracted a situation that gave you a negative reaction at your core? Do you know why you reacted this way?

_____

_____

_____

_____

_____

_____

_____

What are countermeasures you can take to address the triggers you thought of in the previous prompt? What about the things, situations, or people creates a negative trigger? Take any associated thoughts and reframe them positively.

_____

_____

_____

_____

_____

_____

_____

Knowledge is power. For this week's activity, look for ways to learn how to shift your mindset in positive ways. You can read a book, magazine, or blog or listen to an inspiring audiobook or podcast.

PERSONAL SECURITY

*I act from a place of personal security.
I have integrity, I am reliable, and I am
true to my word.*

Personal security is tied to your confidence and how your needs are met. What does personal security mean to you, and how does it manifest to meet your needs?

_____

_____

_____

_____

_____

_____

_____

On a scale of 1 to 10, with 10 being the most positive response, how do you rank your personal security, integrity, reliability, and your word?

_____

_____

_____

_____

_____

_____

_____

Personal security and reliability are connected with our values. How can you continue to positively build on these values?

_____

_____

_____

_____

_____

_____

Today, you are going to create a contract with yourself. In this contract, detail your personal commitment to developing your security, integrity, and reliability to your desired levels. What are your nonnegotiables? Get creative! The contract can be an artistic expression of your personal security, so try adding color or using special paper or throw in some glitter.

COMPARISON FREEDOM

I compare myself only to my highest self.
I choose not to compare myself to others
because everyone is different.

The comparison game is a thinking trap. It creates a false narrative that impacts self-perception. What do you feel makes you unique?

_____

_____

_____

_____

_____

_____

_____

Everyone's journey is different and so it makes no sense to compare; however, everyone is susceptible. What is the biggest lesson you've learned in self-discovery?

_____

_____

_____

_____

_____

_____

_____

Think about your present self and then think about your highest self. Your comparison should only apply to yourself. What would a letter to your higher self look like? How would you express the joy for what you've learned in your personal journey?

_____

_____

_____

_____

_____

_____

Remember the Pinterest board you built on page 52, where you added ways to increase your self-care, confidence, and build on your routine? Today, you will add inspiration to your Pinterest board for where you want your higher self to go. Add visuals that represent your vision for your higher self. You can even add individuals who inspire you.

WEEK 21

SUPPORT SYSTEM

I persevere even when others don't share my dreams. I turn to loved ones who support my efforts.

Having a support system is an important part of life. It can elevate us and push us to new heights. How would you describe your support system?

_____

_____

_____

_____

_____

_____

_____

It is normal for us to be influenced by and aspire to be like others. Is there anyone in your support system who influences you?

_____

_____

_____

_____

_____

_____

_____

A support system can include many things, such as individuals (family, friends, peers), organizations, and routines or processes. What are the ways in which you are supported? Are there ways you can improve your support system?

_____

_____

_____

_____

_____

_____

_____

Today's activity is going to be impactful not just to you but to the individuals who most closely engage as part of your support system. Spend some time developing a plan for how you would like to express gratitude and give thanks to these people for their support. Some ideas include sharing a meal, a simple gift, or a note.

MY FRIENDSHIPS

*My friends accept me for who I am.
My friendships are meaningful,
supportive, rewarding, and founded on
mutual respect and understanding.*

The people you surround yourself with impact who you are and how you engage with others. What kind of individuals would you say your friends are?

_____

_____

_____

_____

_____

_____

_____

Balance in any relationship is important, which requires give and take. In what ways do your close friends enrich your life and in what ways do you believe you enrich theirs?

_____

_____

_____

_____

_____

_____

_____

Sometimes individuals bring toxicity to a relationship and are not worthy of your friendship. Do you have frenemies like this in your life? How would you salvage and improve that relationship? Or would you choose to end it?

_____

_____

_____

_____

_____

_____

_____

Make it a point to spend more time with your friends. Everyone leads a busy life and because of this, it's easy to disregard our close relationships. For today's activity, reach out to your friendship circle and talk about something you have all wanted to do together, then, make a day of it. It will bring you closer.

WEEK 23

HEALTHY RELATIONSHIPS

My relationships with family members, friends, and significant others are healthy and full of understanding and compassion.

If you can't love yourself, how do you expect to love anybody else? What are ten things you love about yourself? What makes you lovable?

_____

_____

_____

_____

_____

_____

_____

Think of the joys and positive experiences that you have had in your current romantic relationship, or, if you are not currently in a romantic relationship, in friendships or in past relationships. How did this relationship make you feel?

_____

_____

_____

_____

_____

_____

_____

Reread the affirmation for this week. How can you continue to nurture relationships that are healthy, long-lasting, and full of compassion and understanding? Think of all the types of relationships you have experienced.

_____

_____

_____

_____

_____

_____

_____

I hope you like arts and crafts. Get a sketchbook or a journal or combine several pieces of construction paper into a book. In your book, write, draw, and create your vision for the manifestation of healthy relationships. Use this to manifest anything in the future that you desire with your relationships.

MOMENTS OF JOY

My life is filled with happiness.
I face each day with the care and
support of those close to me.

Our happy moments tend to become our most cherished memories in life. Everyone should strive to achieve happiness. What is your happiest moment and why?

_____

_____

_____

_____

_____

_____

_____

Using this happy moment, or any other happy moment you can think of, what are some key similarities you can see that are shared among all of your happy experiences?

_____

_____

_____

_____

_____

_____

People should feel fully empowered to create and navigate life moments. Is there anything you are currently experiencing or creating that you are really excited about?

_____

_____

_____

_____

_____

_____

_____

Today, you are going to create a collage or highlight reel of your happy moments. One of the great things about modern technology is that it allows us to easily preserve memories. Create a collage of photos and videos that you can look back on time and again as a way to remind yourself of happy memories.

COMMUNICATION

I communicate my desires, my needs, my wants, and my feelings clearly, boldly, and confidently. I let my voice roam free.

Communication and comprehension are important skills because they relate to how well people understand you and how well you understand others. How do you engage with and communicate your feelings to the people around you?

_____

_____

_____

_____

_____

_____

_____

So much can change in the span of a year. Think about your communication; what has helped you improve it over the year?

_____

_____

_____

_____

_____

_____

_____

What is your greatest asset with the way you engage and express yourself? How do you think others would describe your style of communication?

_____

_____

_____

_____

_____

_____

_____

Many people struggle with communication at times. In fact, many individuals find it nerve-racking to speak on a stage or attempt public speaking. Today, step out of your comfort zone and communicate in a way that is new to you. For example, try speaking on a stage at an event, creating a TikTok video, or making a presentation at work.

WEEK 26

ABUNDANT MIND

I see abundance everywhere I go. I attract prosperity and lucrative opportunities that are in alignment with my needs, wants, and desires.

Breathing is often a subconscious action. It is a function so natural that it does not require focused thought. Gratitude should be done in a similar way. What are you most grateful for?

_____

_____

_____

_____

_____

_____

Think about all the blessings you possess, such as skill, prosperity, and opportunities. How do you see abundance manifest in your life?

_____

_____

_____

_____

_____

_____

People can experience a variety of emotions when they feel like they are lacking. The key is to focus on the positives regardless of the situation. How do you feel when you receive?

_____

_____

_____

_____

_____

_____

_____

Remember the manifestation book you created earlier this year? Today, you are going to add your personal vision statement to that book. This vision statement will outline how you will craft and continue to attract abundance in your life. Be specific about what you want to attract and do not dwell on what you lack.

ATTRACTING ABUNDANCE

I am thankful and grateful for the abundance in my life. I easily and instantly manifest needs, desires, and wants.

In order to manifest and attract needs, desires, and wants, people need to be clear on their ask. What do you want to experience or create in your life? Be specific.

_____

_____

_____

_____

_____

_____

_____

Goals are a form of manifestation. You think about it, plan it, and execute. What goals do you want to accomplish in the next three to six months?

_____

_____

_____

_____

_____

_____

Attraction goes both ways. You can attract positives or negatives. Fear is a big component of this. What are some of the fears impacting abundance in your life?

_____

_____

_____

_____

_____

_____

_____

Today, I want you to take part in a ritual to combat your fears. You are going to write your fears on something and then destroy them. One possible way to accomplish this is to write all your fears on note cards and after reading them aloud, burn them. Or, write your fears with marker on white plates and smash them.

THE JOURNEY

Today is the future I created yesterday.
Tomorrow will be the future I manifest today
and it will be even better than expected.

This week let's celebrate the journey. What are some of your accomplishments that you are most proud of? Nothing is too big or small when it comes to your journey.

_____

_____

_____

_____

_____

_____

_____

Think about your journey to date. What is something you have accomplished, that if you looked back at your younger self, you never could have imagined?

_____

_____

_____

_____

_____

_____

_____

Keeping your journey in mind, and the previous prompts in this book, what would you like to manifest in your life now? What do you envision for your ideal life in the next one to three years?

_____

_____

_____

_____

_____

_____

_____

Celebrations are always in order but more so for today's activity. Think about what you have achieved in your life and ways you can celebrate your accomplishments. Then celebrate them. Ideas for celebration could include a fun photo shoot, a trip, painting night, dinner with a friend, or a low-key event with close loved ones.

WEEK 29

BLESSINGS ABOUND

I enjoy sharing my good fortune. I rejoice for others who are successful, prosperous, and have lives full of abundance.

There are many blessings in people's lives, but people often forget to show gratitude for those blessings. In what ways do you try to show gratitude for the blessings you have received?

_____

_____

_____

_____

_____

_____

_____

Knowing that you have so many blessings, how do you share your good fortune with others? How do you rejoice in the abundance experienced by others and how does it make you feel?

_____

_____

_____

_____

_____

_____

_____

Even if you are not always cognizant of your blessings, you can improve and start showing gratitude today. In what ways can you start showing joy and gratitude for yourself and others and the abundance you experience?

_____

_____

_____

_____

_____

_____

_____

It is important to share and pay forward your blessings. Today, do something to enrich the life of another person. Some ideas include volunteering at a facility that provides emergency housing, giving food to those who need it, or donating money and time to a good cause.

HEALING

My journey is healing and unique. I care for my mind, body, and soul by fulfilling their nourishment needs.

Every individual is on their own journey and no two individuals are alike, which means that the best modalities for healing and care vary from person to person. How do you care for yourself?

_____

_____

_____

_____

_____

_____

_____

Some lessons create a tremendous impact in people's lives that won't soon be forgotten. In your opinion, what has been the greatest lesson you have learned about self-healing?

_____

_____

_____

_____

_____

_____

It's important to nourish the mind, body, and soul. On a scale of 1 to 10, with 10 being the most positive response, how would you rate your self-nourishment? Why?

_____

_____

_____

_____

_____

_____

_____

Communing with nature has many benefits, from pleasing the senses to stimulating the production of feel-good hormones. Today, I want you to plan a hike either solo or with friends that ends with a delicious picnic. If inviting friends, make it more fun by ensuring everyone contributes a different item to the picnic haul.

YOUR CAREER

My work is meaningful and impactful. I take pride in it and perform my duties with the utmost diligence and attention.

What are some of the things you enjoy most about your work? Is it the people, process, or the impact? How does your work make you feel?

_____

_____

_____

_____

_____

_____

_____

As children, thinking and dreaming big comes easily. Aspiration comes naturally. Take a trip down memory lane and remember your childhood dreams. What were your aspirations?

_____

_____

_____

_____

_____

_____

_____

What is something that you have always wanted to do in your career that you haven't done? What is preventing you from doing it?

_____

_____

_____

_____

_____

_____

_____

Channel your inner child's aspirations and the ability to dream big. Children don't think about obstacles or potential failure. Based on your response to the previous prompt, take the next step, even if it's a small one, and move forward on achieving that career goal.

THE IMPACT

I believe in my ability to change and impact the world with what I do. My uniqueness is its own form of magic.

Everyone has their own form of magic and uniqueness. Is there a talent or ability that you have yet to share with the world?

_____

_____

_____

_____

_____

_____

_____

What do you think is the most important thing to remember in your own self-care journey and what do you want to be telling yourself in ten years?

_____

_____

_____

_____

_____

_____

_____

Everyone has their individual self-perception, while others have their perceptions of us. How do you want others to describe you when they are asked?

_____

_____

_____

_____

_____

_____

_____

Create a photo album of all the attributes that make you unique and magical. Make it a chronological album from your youth to now or vice versa. Decorate it as you wish, write in it, and use it when you need reminding of the amazing individual you are. Choose to share it if you wish.

ALIGNMENT

My body, my mind, and my soul are in alignment and support my lifestyle and fulfill my wants, desires, and needs.

Sometimes when people experience difficulty or challenges it is because something is not in alignment with where they are meant to be or where they are going. Where are you experiencing areas of misalignment?

_____

_____

_____

_____

_____

_____

_____

Why are you experiencing the misalignment identified in the previous prompt? What about this dislocation is telling you that you may need a change in direction?

_____

_____

_____

_____

_____

_____

_____

Take a moment to assess and reframe these challenges into a form that is acceptable and in alignment with you. Remember, small steps matter.

_____

_____

_____

_____

_____

_____

Today, I want you to work on aligning your mind. You have various options for how to proceed, but I recommend that you participate in a guided meditation class. You can join a class or follow one of the many options on YouTube.

EMPOWERED ENERGY

I am sexy and desirable. When I look in the mirror I am in awe and in love with the reflection that is looking back at me.

Own your power, desirability, and sexual energy. How did it make you feel to read or recite the previous affirmation? Make note of the emotion and the physical manifestation in your body.

_____

_____

_____

_____

_____

_____

_____

Diving a bit deeper, explore the emotion that this affirmation has brought up in you, as well as the physical manifestation in your body. Why do you think this is the reaction you're having?

_____

_____

_____

_____

_____

_____

_____

What types of things help you feel empowered, desirable, and sexual?

_____

_____

_____

_____

_____

_____

_____

Create a list of powerful phrases and affirmations that empower you to embrace your power, desirability, and sexual nature. Once you do, stand in front of your mirror and recite your list aloud to yourself. Make it fun by creating a vibe that gets you in this space. Try incorporating a piece of clothing that makes you feel like a badass.

WEEK 35

LESSONS LEARNED

*I am not defined by my mistakes. I see mistakes
as learning experiences to help me overcome
the next challenge.*

What is your thought process for overcoming major challenges or difficulties? Does this vary based on the type of challenge or difficulty?

_____

_____

_____

_____

_____

_____

_____

Think back to a time when you made a big mistake. What lessons did you learn? What growth did you experience through this mistake?

_____

_____

_____

_____

_____

_____

_____

Mistakes are opportunities for growth and should not define anyone. What are the most valuable lessons you have learned from your mistakes? How do you apply these lessons in your life today?

_____

_____

_____

_____

_____

_____

_____

Mindset is key when dealing with anything in life. Explore ways to further your mindset outside of the work you are doing within this journal. Research courses on mindset transformation and positive thinking, then schedule some time to take part in the course. It will be life changing.

WEEK 36

HIGHER SELF

I engage in work and seek opportunities
that are in alignment with my higher self.
I have a vision for the impact I want to
make in the world.

Individuals should always strive to be better than they were yesterday. To that end, what are the things you do to ensure that you are continually evolving?

_____

_____

_____

_____

_____

_____

_____

Every person is unique, and so is their perception and vision of their higher self. When you think about your higher self and the impact you want to make in the world, how do you feel?

_____

_____

_____

_____

_____

_____

In relation to the impact you want to make in the world, coupled with the things that bring you joy, what would you like for your future higher self to be doing more of?

_____

_____

_____

_____

_____

_____

_____

You're ninety years old, looking back on your life and writing a letter to your younger self in which you are apologizing for all the opportunities you missed. What missed opportunities would you include? The great thing about writing this letter is that you can correct your course now and make the necessary changes in your life.

CAREER AND PASSION

I love all of the work that I do. My workplace is full of contagious praise, peace, and enthusiasm.

There is a saying that goes, "If your work is something you love, you'll never work a day in your life." How does that sentence make you feel when you think about your workplace?

_____

_____

_____

_____

_____

_____

Culture is important in the workplace. In what ways do your work colleagues provide support, praise, peace, and enthusiasm to you? How do you contribute to the environment?

_____

_____

_____

_____

_____

_____

What are the things you would love to be doing more of in your career? What is stopping you from doing those things and what would you need to do to remove any hurdles?

_____

_____

_____

_____

_____

_____

_____

Reach out to your colleagues and compare their workplace perception to yours. Discuss the ways you can foster inclusion, praise, peace, and activities that will boost morale and create contagious enthusiasm. Then determine how you can make it happen.

PRIORITIZING YOU

I make the commitment to give to others what I want to receive. I make the conscious choice to put myself first.

Relationships, regardless of the type of relationship, should be reciprocal. Ever hear the phrase that you can't pour from an empty cup? How do you protect your energy and keep your cup full?

_____

_____

_____

_____

_____

_____

_____

Part of self-care is ensuring that you prioritize yourself. Believe it or not, this is something many people put on the back burner. In what ways do you prioritize yourself?

_____

_____

_____

_____

_____

_____

_____

What are the practices you put in place, or can put in place, to ensure that other individuals pour into you as much as you pour into them?

_____

_____

_____

_____

_____

_____

_____

Today, do something fun just for yourself. It is more than okay for you to spend time reenergizing yourself by doing things that invigorate you and make you feel joy. Today, you have a date with yourself. Buy yourself some flowers or a sweet treat or take a road trip.

PRESENT AWARENESS

I choose to participate fully in my day. I choose to be present. I choose what emotions to give power to.

You may sometimes find yourself going through the motions or navigating on autopilot. In moments like these, what brings your awareness back to the present?

_____

_____

_____

_____

_____

_____

_____

To increase gratitude, it's important to enjoy simple pleasures. Think about your day-to-day life. What moments do you enjoy the most? What types of feelings do these moments evoke for you?

_____

_____

_____

_____

_____

_____

_____

Emotions are powerful and can deeply impact mood, personality, and action. How do you positively deal with difficult emotions currently? What can you do in the future to positively deal with emotions?

_____

_____

_____

_____

_____

_____

Believe it or not, the physical state of your body can help you move out of a slump, positively improve your mood, or stir happy memories. Research physiology and ways you can put your body into a positive physical state. That way when you need a boost you can rely on this practice.

SOLUTIONING

I take a break and allow my subconscious to help me find the answers to my problems as I look at them from multiple angles.

Sometimes you can get stuck reliving, rehashing, or problem-solving a situation. When this happens, sometimes you may need to take a break and come back refreshed. When was a time you stepped away in order to get a fresh perspective? Did stepping away help?

_____

_____

_____

_____

_____

_____

_____

What useful things can you do when you step away from trying to find a solution to a problem?

_____

_____

_____

_____

_____

_____

_____

Is there anything you have seen others do or any feedback others have provided on what helps them in these moments? Anything you would like to try?

_____

_____

_____

_____

_____

_____

_____

Our brains are powerhouses of information, but the brain requires exercise. Today, play games, work on a crossword puzzle, or engage in logic puzzles to stimulate your mind. There are plenty of free resources online, mobile apps, and even books you can purchase.

COURAGE

I face difficulties with courage. I believe in my ability to find and navigate the path that is right for me.

Take a moment to reflect and write about an experience that had a profound impact on your life. How did that event impact your character and perception?

_____

_____

_____

_____

_____

_____

Courage can take on different meanings for different people depending on their life experiences and perception. What does courage mean to you, and how has it helped you navigate difficulties in your life?

_____

_____

_____

_____

_____

_____

Trusting your abilities is important. What strategies do you implement to build your character, manage reactions, develop emotional stability, and solve challenges?

_____

_____

_____

_____

_____

_____

_____

There is always a learning curve with anything new. Make a list of situations in which you lacked confidence or didn't trust your abilities. Then, take the steps to overcome your lack of confidence. For example, if you're interested in roller-skating but scared about injury, take a class to increase your confidence.

VALIDATION

I release the need to feel the validation of others. I require no one's input or approval except my own.

If motivation toward a goal is lacking, having a strong foundation to carry you forward is important. What are several of your goals and the driving force helping you go after them?

_____

_____

_____

_____

_____

_____

_____

It is very easy to fall into the trap of wanting validation from others, especially with the influence of society and social media. What steps can you take to diminish the need for external validation?

_____

_____

_____

_____

_____

_____

_____

No one's input or approval should matter more than your own. When have you felt the need for external validation? How would you rewrite those situations now with a focus on only your own self-validation?

_____

_____

_____

_____

_____

_____

_____

Seek to empower yourself in order to create opportunities for joy, laughter, and self-acceptance. Surround yourself with individuals who will uplift you and add to your cup rather than deplete it. Research groups in your area for confidence, empowerment, and support. Consider joining one.

NEGATIVE ENERGY

I choose to free myself from all the negativity and energy that attempt to impede or block my progress and growth.

You may have heard of energy vampires. They are people who drain your energy and leave you fatigued. Is this something you experience, and how do you handle the aftermath?

_____

_____

_____

_____

_____

_____

_____

Do you have areas in your life where you are experiencing negativity or blockages that are impeding your progress and growth? How can you reduce or remove those blocks?

_____

_____

_____

_____

_____

_____

_____

There are many ways to relax and shift your mood so that you can positively impact your physical body. When you are feeling drained or focusing too much on negativity, what can you do to shift toward the positive?

_____

_____

_____

_____

_____

_____

_____

Our senses greatly impact and shape our experiences and memory. For example, our sense of smell has a powerful impact on our feelings and memories. Take an excursion today and seek out scents that you find pleasing and that positively alter your mood. Find a way to bring them into your space.

WEEK 44

JOY IN THE PRESENT

My heart is full of joy. I look at the world around me and can't help but smile and feel joy.

There are opportunities for beauty, happiness, and abundance if you know where to look. What is one thing that has made you incredibly happy recently? Describe the depth of emotion.

_____

_____

_____

_____

_____

_____

_____

Reflect on the things around you. What are the things in your environment, home, work, community that bring you joy? How can you build more time into your schedule for appreciating these things?

_____

_____

_____

_____

_____

_____

_____

What are the things you are doing in your life to increase your joy and abundance? Be as specific as possible and make note of opportunities to enhance this further.

_____

_____

_____

_____

_____

_____

_____

Today, focus on the things that bring you the most joy. Plan a day for yourself with all the activities you enjoy the most. Your favorite outfit, favorite food, favorite places, basically anything that brings you true happiness and spend the day enjoying those things. It's all about bringing in more joy and creating positive memories.

SELF-SOOTHING

*I have all the support and help I need.
I gain valuable insights from my
experiences in any given situation.*

It is important to be able to self-soothe when necessary. What do you like to do when you are feeling down or stressed? How does this activity alter your state of mind?

_____

_____

_____

_____

_____

_____

_____

Each individual handles things in the way that works best for them. Having a support system is very useful. How do you ensure that you have the proper or adequate support?

_____

_____

_____

_____

_____

_____

Insight and inspiration can come from the unlikeliest of places. What is the most inspiring thing you have seen or done in the last two weeks?

_____

_____

_____

_____

_____

_____

_____

Today, you are going to make use of the manifestation book you created earlier in your journal practice. Remember, you can use your book at any time to help you manifest your desires. Add to your book and fill it with motivational and inspirational content to drive your aspirations and growth.

PHYSICAL MANIFESTATION

I release my mind of negative thoughts and I let go of the worries that can drain my excitement and energy.

Negative thoughts and stress can manifest in your body in many ways. What does it mean to you to have no worries or stress about the future?

_____

_____

_____

_____

_____

_____

_____

Reflect on the moments when you have experienced a great deal of stress. How did it manifest in your mind and body and what tactics did you use to address the stress?

_____

_____

_____

_____

_____

_____

_____

It is important to address and identify the things that can trigger a negative or stressful response. What do you find to be your triggers for stress?

_____

_____

_____

_____

_____

_____

_____

There are many ways to deal with negative thoughts and stress. In fact, you have been engaging in such a practice through your journaling. Communing with nature and visiting your favorite places is a way to deal with stress and invoke good feelings. Today, visit your favorite location for positive inspiration.

MIND AND BODY

*I have the ability to rise above challenges.
I am calm, I am happy, I am content,
and I am at peace.*

You are capable, but that doesn't mean you have to journey alone. When you are upset, do you prefer to talk with someone, or do you prefer alone time?

_____

_____

_____

_____

_____

_____

_____

Alignment in mind and body can bring about many benefits. What have you done today to align your physical form with your mental state?

_____

_____

_____

_____

_____

_____

Individuals are influenced in many ways. Do you feel like your race or culture has influenced your thoughts and how you engage in the world?

_____

_____

_____

_____

_____

_____

Today, make a plan to create a routine or sequence that soothes you when you are feeling unlike yourself. Whenever you feel overwhelmed or stressed or are experiencing something akin to imposter syndrome, do something good for both your mind and body. It might be drinking herbal tea, journaling, or doing yoga: whatever speaks to you and is in alignment with your values.

WEEK 48

BEYOND RISK

Every choice I make leads to bigger and better opportunities. The answer is before me if I look carefully at the details.

It is not uncommon to feel apprehensive or fearful when faced with uncertainty. Uncertainty can derail decision-making. How do you move past analysis paralysis so that you're able to make a decision?

_____

_____

_____

_____

_____

_____

_____

Every action and decision has a cause and effect, and this can drive fear and apprehension when making decisions. What are some activities you can add to your routine to address analysis paralysis?

_____

_____

_____

_____

_____

_____

_____

There can be risks in making decisions. Some people welcome risk and others are averse to it. Where do you fall on the spectrum of acceptance of or aversion to risk?

_____

_____

_____

_____

_____

_____

_____

Take a chance on yourself today. Invest in yourself regardless of the risk. Do something that you might be hesitant to try because of the perceived risk. Want to start a YouTube channel, podcast, or blog? Today is the day to go for it.

A FULL LIFE

I do my best to model the type of life I want to lead, a life full of love, peace, abundance, and happiness.

Perception is unique to the individual. Your vision of a good or model life might be different from that of the next person. What does it mean to you to live a good life?

_____

_____

_____

_____

_____

_____

_____

It is okay to want more while at the same time being grateful and appreciative of what you have. Are there things about your life you want to improve upon?

_____

_____

_____

_____

_____

_____

_____

Repeat this week's affirmation. What does it mean to you to have a life full of love, peace, abundance, and happiness?

_____

_____

_____

_____

_____

_____

_____

Reshaping negative thoughts and habits into something positive takes time, effort, and belief. It's important to create a belief and support system to carry you forward in your journey. Today, create an affirmation for each of the following: love, peace, abundance, and happiness.

MINDFUL CHANGES

I feel calmness and confidence wash over me with every deep breath I take. With each breath I become more centered and grounded.

Close your eyes and slowly count to ten, inhaling and exhaling every other count. Repeat a second time while focusing on your breath. How do you feel?

_____

_____

_____

_____

_____

_____

_____

Earlier in your journaling journey you were tasked with exploring meditation and other mindfulness activities to shift your thoughts to the positive. How has this practice affected you? Have you combined meditation with other practices?

_____

_____

_____

_____

_____

_____

Growth and learning are continuous and they can enrich your life. In what ways has your thinking changed in the last year with your journaling practice? What positive habits have you developed?

_____

_____

_____

_____

_____

_____

Incorporate a change of scenery into your favorite mind-fulness activity. Practice in a location that is new to you, such as an outdoor yoga or breath class, or look into some health and wellness retreats that interest you.

POSITIVE STATE

I am grounded in my positivity. I can access and tap into a wellspring of inner happiness anytime that I wish.

Read that affirmation again. What are a few of the happiest memories you have from different periods of your life?

_____

_____

_____

_____

_____

_____

_____

This year you have worked hard to build positive habits. What do you feel has been most useful to you in developing these habits? What has helped you the most and the least?

_____

_____

_____

_____

_____

_____

_____

It is important that you continue to develop your positive state and build on the habits you've put in place. What are you most excited about in regards to your continued development?

_____

_____

_____

_____

_____

_____

_____

Today, work on creating your highlight reel. Reflect on the positive change and the times you felt inspired this past year. When did you feel most inspired? Now, create a vision board, list, or collage of all the positive moments you have experienced from your journaling practice.

CONTINUED GROWTH

I have grown and developed positive habits. I choose myself and promise myself to continue evolving my positivity practice.

This past year has been a long road and at times, came with its challenges. But guess what? You made it! Think back to the day you started journaling versus today. How did you feel when you started and how do you feel today? What has changed most for you?

_____

_____

_____

_____

_____

_____

_____

What are the one or two things you have learned in your fifty-two-week journaling practice? How would you go about teaching others what you learned?

_____

_____

_____

_____

_____

_____

_____

Thank yourself. In what ways can you express gratitude for all your hard work and time investment in your personal development? Be specific.

_____

_____

_____

_____

_____

_____

_____

Celebration is in order! You made the commitment to partake in this fifty-two-week journal practice and in doing so, you have developed habits and the foundation to shift your thoughts toward the positive. That is no small feat and so you should celebrate in a way that resonates with you. Be proud of yourself.

A FINAL WORD

Congratulations! You did it.

You've completed the entire journal, and hopefully you've found the process rewarding. You've learned lots of new techniques for positive thinking and journaling, and you should feel proud of yourself. Now that you have these new skills, there are several ways you can put them to use in your life. For example:

- Expand your writing practice to a daily gratitude list or a weekly recap of your accomplishments.

- Try new avenues for creativity, like coloring books or karaoke.

- Take up a new hobby or activity, one that helps you relax or give back to others. I recommend volunteering at a local animal shelter.

- Share what you've learned with friends and family who might benefit from learning more about positive thinking—it's good to have an accountability partner when learning something new.

Keep in mind these positive thinking practices as you go through your day:

- Recognize when negative thoughts pop into your head and try to reframe them as positives. Instead of thinking, "I'll never get this done," try thinking, "I'm going to do my best."

- Remember that being overly critical of yourself isn't helpful. Cut yourself some slack, and remember that everyone makes mistakes.

- Remind yourself of all the things you've accomplished so far. You've gotten this far because you're awesome.

No matter what you decide to do next, I hope this journal has set the stage for a lifetime of positivity. I wish you the best as you continue on your journey.

RESOURCES

BOOKS FOR POSITIVITY AND MINDSET SHIFTS

The Gifts of Imperfection by Brené Brown

The Power of Positive Thinking by Dr. Norman Vincent Peale

Rewire Your Brain by Jacob King

PODCASTS FOR POSITIVITY AND MINDSET SHIFTS

Happier with Gretchen Rubin by Gretchen Rubin

Positivity Podcast by Paul McKenna

She is Fab by Evelyn Betances

WEBSITES FOR POSITIVITY AND MINDSET SHIFTS

Happify, happify.com

The Happiness Project, the-happiness-project.com

100 Happy Days, 100happydays.com

1000 Awesome Things (blog), 1000awesomethings.com

REFERENCES

Boom Positive. "Positive Verbs: List from A to Z 'Action Words.'"
boompositive.com/pages/list-of-positive-verbs-a-to-z.

Borge, Jonathan. "40 Positive Affirmations to Add to Your Daily
Rotation." Oprah Daily. oprahdaily.com/life/relationships-love/
g25629970/positive-affirmations.

Dreher, Diane. "Creating Positive Life Changes." VIA Institute on
Character. viacharacter.org/topics/articles/creating-positive-life
-changes.

Lindsay, Emily K., and J. David Creswell. "Helping the Self Help
Others: Self-Affirmation Increases Self-Compassion and
Pro-Social Behaviors." *Frontiers in Psychology*. May 12, 2014.
frontiersin.org/articles/10.3389/fpsyg.2014.00421/full.

Mind Tools Content Team. "The Power of Good Habits: Using
High-Performance Habits to Achieve Your Goals." mindtools
.com/pages/article/power-good-habits.htm.

Rebecca. "20 Positive Changes You Can Make Right Now."
Minimalism Made Simple. February 17, 2021.
minimalismmadesimple.com/home/positive-changes.

Waters, Shonna. "50 Good Habits to Help Spur Your Mental
Well-Being." *BetterUp* (blog). August 31, 2021. betterup.com
/blog/good-habits.

ABOUT THE AUTHOR

 **Evelyn Betances** is a speaker, strategist, and mindset transformation coach. She is the founder and CEO of the Fab Chieftess, a brand whose purpose is to inform and inspire individuals to reclaim their authority, boost confidence, address impostor syndrome, and overcome fear so that they can bring their aspirations to life. She works with people from all walks of life to help them harness the power of mindset, personalized self-care, accountability, and strategy. As a mindset practitioner and coach, she believes that investment in your growth does not have to be complicated or expensive, but it does have to be intentional.

CPSIA information can be obtained
at www.ICGtesting.com
Printed in the USA
JSHW041245071022
31426JS00001B/1